Tips for Talking and Reading Together

Stories are a fun and reassuring way of introducing children to new experiences.

- Talk about the title and the pictures on the cover.
- Talk about your child's expectations and emotions.
- Read the story with your child.
- Have fun finding the hidden bones.

When you've read the story:

- Discuss the Talk About ideas on page 27.
- Look at the pictures and vocabulary on pages 28–29.
- Have fun finding the objects in the pictures.
- Do the fun activity at the end.

Have fun!

Find the bone hidden in every picture.

At the Vet

Roderick Hunt • Annemarie Young

Alex Brychta

OXFORD

UNIVERSITY PRESS

Floppy chased a rabbit. The rabbit ran under a fence. Floppy went under the fence too, but he got stuck.

Dad ran to help Floppy. "Oh no!"
he said. "I think Floppy has cut
himself."

Dad looked at the cut. "Sorry
Floppy," he said. "It's a deep cut.
We must take you to the vet."

The children were upset. They all
wanted to go to the vet with Floppy.
"Poor Floppy," said Kipper.

They went to the vet. Some people were waiting. "That dog needs to see the vet first," said a man.

"Yes," said a lady. "Let him go
first. My snake can wait."

The vet cleaned Floppy's cut.
"It will need stitches," she said.

Kipper was worried. "Will it hurt
him?" he asked.

"No," said the vet. "He won't feel anything. We'll check him over and then we'll help him go to sleep."

"Will he be all right?" asked Biff.

"He'll be fine," said the vet.
"Give him a big hug, then you can
go home. When he wakes up, you
can come and get him."

The children gave Floppy a hug.

"Poor old Floppy," said Chip.

Floppy had the stitches and he
soon woke up. The children came
with Dad to take him home.

Floppy tried to chew his stitches.
"We can't let him do that," said
the vet.

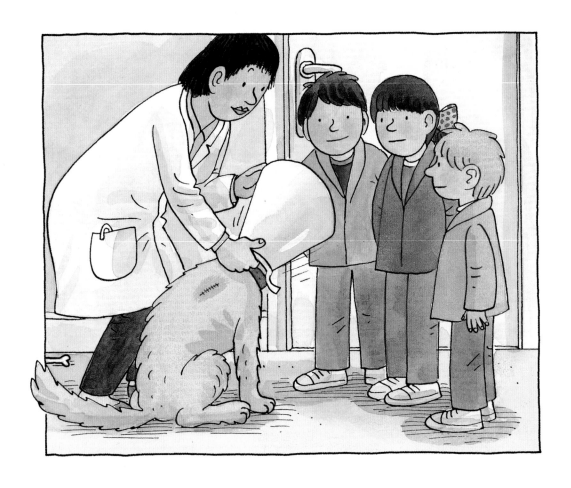

The vet put a cone collar on
Floppy. "He mustn't chew the
stitches," she said. "This will stop
him from chewing."

"Poor Floppy!" said Kipper. "The collar looks like a lampshade."

They took Floppy home, but he
didn't like the cone collar.

CRASH! He knocked over
the plants. BUMP! He ran into
doorways. THUMP! He knocked
into the children's legs.

Kipper had an idea. "Let's put this on him instead," he said.

They put Kipper's old top on
Floppy. He still couldn't chew his
stitches, but he didn't seem to mind.

Floppy liked Kipper's top.

"It's better than a cone collar,"
said Kipper.

22

Floppy's cut was soon better.
He went back to the vet to have his
stitches out.

The vet checked Floppy's cut.
"It's healed very well," she said.

She let Kipper listen to Floppy's
heart. "He's fine," she said. "Floppy
is very fit."

"He's as good as new," said the vet.
"But my old top isn't!" said Kipper.

Talk about the story

Why were the children worried when Floppy cut himself?

Why did Floppy have to have stitches?

How did Kipper feel at the end of the story?

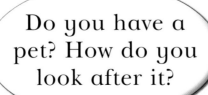

Do you have a pet? How do you look after it?

What do you find at the vet?

Talk about the things you see on this page. Can you think of anything else you might find at the vet?

Now look back at the story and find these things in the pictures.

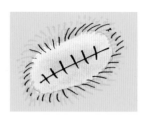

stitches

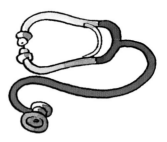

stethoscope

antiseptic

sick pet

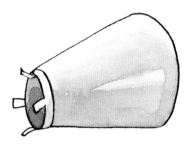

cone collar

clippers

thermometer

cat box

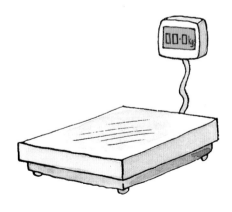

weighing scales

A Maze

Help the rabbit find its burrow.

First Experiences

At the Vet
Roderick Hunt • Alex Brychta
F·I·R·S·T E·X·P·E·R·I·E·N·C·E·S

At the Dentist
Roderick Hunt • Alex Brychta
F·I·R·S·T E·X·P·E·R·I·E·N·C·E·S

At School
Roderick Hunt • Alex Brychta
F·I·R·S·T E·X·P·E·R·I·E·N·C·E·S

At the Pool
Roderick Hunt • Alex Brychta
F·I·R·S·T E·X·P·E·R·I·E·N·C·E·S

Books for children to read and enjoy

The Snowman
Cynthia Rider • Alex Brychta

Super Dad
Roderick Hunt • Alex Brychta

Dragon Danger
Cynthia Rider • Alex Brychta

Arctic Adventure
Roderick Hunt • Alex Brychta

The Hairy-Scary Monster
Cynthia Rider • Alex Brychta

Level 1: Getting Ready

Level 2: Starting to Read

Level 3: Becoming a Reader

Level 4: Building Confidence

Level 5: Reading with Confidence

OXFORD
UNIVERSITY PRESS

Great Clarendon Street,
Oxford OX2 6DP

Text © Roderick Hunt and
Annemarie Young 2007
Illustrations © Alex Brychta 2007

First published 2007
All rights reserved

Series Editors: Kate Ruttle, Annemarie Young

British Library Cataloguing in Publication Data available

ISBN: 978-019-838656-8
With thanks to Haidee Barkar MRCVS and Jonathan
Horrocks MRCVS

10 9 8 7 6 5 4 3 2 1

Printed in China by Imago